CYNTHIA UHL

Kauai: Traveling on a Budget

Complete guide to visiting Kauai on a budget

First edition

This book was professionally typeset on Reedsy.
Find out more at reedsy.com

To my loving family an ocean away.

The mountains are calling and I must go.

- JOHN MUIR

Contents

Introduction

Welcome to KAUAI: TRAVELING ON A BUDGET - Complete guide to visiting Kauai on a budget. Whether you're a family seeking adventure, a solo traveler looking to explore, or a group of friends wanting to experience the best of Kauai without breaking the bank, this guide is your go-to resource for an unforgettable Hawaiian vacation.

Kauai, known as the "Garden Isle," is renowned for its stunning landscapes, from lush rain forests and dramatic cliffs to pristine beaches and vibrant local culture. But while the island's natural beauty is captivating, planning a trip on a budget can seem challenging. That's where this guide comes in. Written with cost-conscious travelers in mind, it provides practical, no-nonsense advice on how to enjoy Kauai to the fullest while sticking to a budget of $3000 or less.

Why This Book?

As someone who has explored Kauai extensively, visited many times, and currently has family living there, I understand the desire to experience all that this island paradise has to offer without overspending. My goal with this book is to give you a clear, concise, and actionable road map to help you plan and execute your trip efficiently. From finding the best budget-friendly accommodations and dining options to uncovering the island's top hikes and activities, this guide covers it all.

What You'll Find in This Guide

Practical Planning Tips:

Before you even set foot on the island, you'll need to plan. The opening chapters will guide you through essential pre-trip details like booking flights, budgeting, packing, and understanding Kauai's weather. You'll learn how to find the best deals on flights, the importance of travel insurance, and what to pack for both beach and mountain adventures. We'll also discuss the nuances of traveling to Kauai from outside the US, including visa requirements and traveling with pets.

Affordable Accommodations:

Once you arrive, where you stay can significantly impact your budget. We'll explore a range of affordable accommodation options, from vacation rentals and hostels to budget hotels and camping sites. You'll get tips on finding the best deals, how to choose accommodations that fit your needs, and strategies for booking early to secure the best rates.

Transportation Options:

Getting around Kauai doesn't have to be expensive. This guide will help you navigate your transportation choices, whether you're considering renting a car, using public transportation, or opting for ride-sharing services. You'll find detailed advice on the most cost-effective and convenient ways to travel around the island, so you can explore without overspending.

Must-See Attractions and Activities:

Kauai is full of incredible sights and activities, many of which are free or low-cost. We'll delve into the island's best beaches, hikes, and day trips, offering recommendations for family-friendly activities and budget-friendly adventures. From scenic coastal drives to hidden waterfalls, you'll discover how to experience the island's highlights without breaking the bank.

Dining on a Budget:

Eating well while traveling can be one of the biggest expenses, but it doesn't have to be. We'll introduce you to affordable dining options, including local eateries and markets where you can enjoy delicious Hawaiian cuisine without spending a fortune. Plus, learn tips on how to save on food costs by cooking some of your own meals and where to find the best deals.

Local Insights and Cultural Tips:

Experiencing Kauai isn't just about sightseeing; it's also about immersing yourself in local culture. This guide provides insights into Hawaiian customs and etiquette, helping you to engage respectfully with the community and enhance your travel experience. You'll gain an understanding of local traditions and cultural practices that make Kauai unique.

How to Use This Guide

This book is designed to be your practical companion throughout your trip planning and travel experience. Each chapter offers step-by-step advice and actionable tips to help you make informed decisions and get the most out of your time in Kauai. Whether you're reading it cover to cover or jumping to specific sections as needed, you'll find the information organized and easy to follow.

By focusing on what truly matters—finding the best deals, making the most of your time, and experiencing Kauai's natural and cultural wonders—this guide ensures that you can enjoy a memorable and affordable Hawaiian getaway. Now, let's dive into the details and start planning your dream trip to Kauai!

With this foundation laid, we'll move on to the first chapter, which will cover essential pre-trip planning and what you need to know before you go. This includes booking flights, budgeting, and preparing for the unique aspects of traveling to Kauai. Ready to start your journey? Let's get going!

1

Pre-Trip Planning and What to Expect

Booking Your Flights

When planning a budget-friendly trip to Kauai, securing the best flight deals can make a significant difference to your overall travel expenses. Start your search well in advance—ideally six months before your intended departure. This allows you to monitor prices and take advantage of any fare drops. Using flight comparison tools like Google Flights, Kayak, or Skyscanner allows you to compare prices across different airlines and set up alerts for when prices drop.

If your travel dates are flexible, you can save even more. Mid-week flights, especially on Tuesdays and Wednesdays, tend to be cheaper due to lower demand. Red-eye flights or those with longer layovers can also offer lower prices, though they might require a bit more patience. Be on the lookout for sales or promotional fares that airlines sometimes offer, particularly during off-peak seasons.

Kauai's main airport, Lihue Airport (LIH), is small but well-equipped, providing travelers with essential amenities like Wi-Fi, food outlets, and car rental services. While you won't find the extensive range of dining and shopping options available at larger airports, you can grab a quick bite or pick up last-minute items before heading out. Keep in mind that LIH doesn't have many late-night flights, so if your arrival is late, plan your transportation and accommodations accordingly.

When budgeting for your flights, expect round-trip fares from the U.S. mainland to Kauai to range from $400 to $800 per person, depending on the time of year and your departure city. Booking early increases your chances of finding fares on the lower end of this range. For international travelers, flights might range from $800 to $1,500 or more, depending on the departure location and season. Booking a multi-leg journey with a stopover on the mainland can sometimes reduce costs.

Once you've booked your flight, consider additional costs like baggage fees, which can add up if you're traveling with more than one checked bag. Some airlines, like Southwest, offer discounted or free checked bags as part of their loyalty programs, so it's worth checking if you're a frequent flier. Also, think about purchasing travel insurance, especially if your trip involves multiple connections or non-refundable bookings. This small investment can provide peace of mind and protect you against unforeseen disruptions.

Arriving from Outside the US

If you're traveling to Kauai from outside the United States, there are a few important steps and considerations to ensure a smooth arrival. First and foremost, make sure your passport is up-to-date and has at least six months of validity beyond your planned departure date. This is a common requirement for international travel, and some airlines may deny boarding if your passport doesn't meet this criterion. Additionally, check whether you need a visa to enter the U.S. If you're from a country participating in the Visa Waiver Program (VWP), you can travel to Hawaii for up to 90 days without a visa, but you'll need to apply for an Electronic System for Travel Authorization (ESTA) at least 72 hours before departure.

When booking your flights, you'll likely find that most international routes to Kauai involve a layover at a major U.S. hub, such as Los Angeles (LAX) or San Francisco (SFO). During your layover, you'll need to go through U.S. Customs and Border Protection (CBP). Be prepared to show your passport, ESTA approval, or visa, and answer routine questions about your trip. Depending on the time of day and the airport, the customs process can take anywhere from 30 minutes to over an hour, so plan your connecting flights with enough time to avoid missing your connection.

If you're traveling with pets, be aware that Hawaii has strict animal quarantine laws to protect its unique ecosystem. Before your pet can enter Kauai, it must meet specific requirements, including rabies vaccinations and a waiting period. Pets must also undergo a health screening and receive a permit from the Hawaii Department of Agriculture. Failure to comply with these regulations can result in your pet being quarantined for up to 120 days, so it's essential to plan ahead if you intend to bring your furry friend.

Another important aspect to consider is the potential for travel disruptions, such as flight delays or cancellations. Purchasing comprehensive travel insurance that covers international flights, medical emergencies, and trip cancellations can be a wise investment. This is especially true if you're connecting through multiple airports, as missing one flight could result in significant delays and additional costs.

Once you arrive at Lihue Airport (LIH), the customs process should be relatively straightforward if you've cleared U.S. customs at your entry point on the mainland. However, it's still important to declare any agricultural products or other restricted items, as Hawaii has strict regulations to prevent the introduction of invasive species.

Budgeting for Your Trip

Creating a realistic budget is essential for enjoying your trip to Kauai without worrying about unexpected expenses. Start by setting a total budget—say $3000—and then break it down into categories such as flights, accommodations, food, activities, transportation, and miscellaneous expenses. This approach ensures that you allocate enough funds for each part of your trip while leaving room for surprises.

When budgeting for accommodations, remember that costs can vary widely depending on the time of year and location. Consider the potential need for last-minute bookings, which can be more expensive. Booking well in advance and opting for budget-friendly options like vacation rentals or hostels can help keep costs down. However, it's wise to set aside a small buffer in your accommodation budget for any unexpected changes, such as a room not being available or needing to switch locations.

Transportation is another key factor. While renting a car provides the most flexibility, it's also one of the larger expenses. Gas prices on Kauai are higher than on the mainland, so factor that into your budget. Public transportation, like the Kauai Bus, is more affordable but less convenient, especially if you plan to explore remote areas. Consider whether you might need extra funds for taxis or ride-sharing services if you decide not to rent a car.

Food is often an overlooked expense. While it's tempting to eat out at every meal, this can quickly add up. A budget of $100-$150 per day for food is reasonable, but you can save by cooking some of your meals if your accommodation has a kitchen. Farmers' markets are a great place to pick up fresh, affordable produce, and you can also enjoy the experience of eating local.

Activities are another significant expense, especially if you plan to do tours or rent equipment like surfboards or snorkeling gear. Many of Kauai's best experiences, like hiking or visiting beaches, are free, but tours, guided hikes, and adventure activities like zip-lining can quickly eat into your budget. Consider prioritizing a few must-do activities and balancing them with free or low-cost experiences.

It's also wise to budget for small but necessary purchases that you might overlook when packing. Items like sunscreen, insect repellent, or even a good pair of hiking shoes can be more expensive on the island. Consider bringing these from home to avoid paying a premium once you're there.

By carefully planning and budgeting for both expected and unexpected expenses, you'll be able to fully enjoy your time in Kauai without worrying about overspending. Remember to review your budget regularly during your trip, adjusting as needed to stay on track.

Weather

Kauai's tropical climate is a dream for many travelers, offering warm temperatures year-round. However, the island's weather can be unpredictable, with sudden rain showers and varying conditions depending on where you are. To make the most of your trip, it's important to understand Kauai's weather patterns and be prepared for changes.

Kauai is known for its microclimates, meaning that weather can vary significantly across different parts of the island. The North Shore, including areas like Hanalei and Princeville, tends to receive more rain, particularly in the winter months from November to March. In contrast, the South Shore, where Poipu is located, is generally sunnier and drier. The East Coast (Coconut Coast) and the West Side (Waimea) also have their own weather quirks, with the West Side being the driest overall.

Rain is a regular part of life on Kauai, so it's essential to pack accordingly. Bring lightweight, breathable clothing that dries quickly, as well as a waterproof jacket or poncho. An umbrella is handy, though wind can sometimes make it challenging to use. For footwear, consider packing waterproof shoes or sandals that can handle wet conditions, especially if you plan to hike. Even if you're visiting during the drier summer months, it's wise to be prepared for the occasional shower, particularly if you're spending time in the lush, green areas of the island.

Kauai is prone to natural phenomena such as flash floods, especially during heavy rains. The island's steep terrain can cause rivers and streams to rise quickly, creating hazardous conditions. It's crucial to be aware of your surroundings, particularly when hiking near streams or waterfalls. Avoid hiking in areas prone to flooding during heavy rain, and never cross flooded roads or trails.

To stay informed about weather conditions and potential natural disasters, sign up for local emergency alerts. The County of Kauai offers a free notification system, Kauai Emergency Management Agency (KEMA), which sends out text and email alerts for severe weather, floods, and other emergencies. Additionally, downloading a weather app like NOAA Weather Radar or the FEMA app can keep you updated on current conditions and warnings.

Hurricane season in Hawaii runs from June to November, though Kauai is rarely directly hit. Still, it's wise to monitor the forecast if you're visiting during these months. Most accommodations will have an emergency plan in place, but it's good practice to familiarize yourself with evacuation routes and procedures, just in case.

What to Pack

Packing for Kauai requires a balance between beach essentials and gear suitable for the island's diverse terrain. Whether you're lounging on a sunny shore or exploring rugged mountain trails, having the right items will ensure you're prepared for all the adventures Kauai has to offer.

For beach days, start with the basics: swimwear, a wide-brimmed hat, and sunglasses with UV protection. The Hawaiian sun can be intense, some high-SPF, reef-safe sunscreen is a must to protect your skin and the environment. Consider packing a lightweight beach cover-up such as a sarong or rash guard to shield yourself from the sun when you're not in the water. A quick-dry towel is also handy, especially if you're hopping from one beach to another or taking a dip before heading to a new destination.

Given Kauai's sandy and often rocky beaches, sturdy water shoes or sandals with good traction are highly recommended. These will protect your feet from sharp coral and give you the grip you need when walking on slippery rocks or exploring tide pools. A waterproof bag or dry sack is another essential item, perfect for keeping your belongings dry and sand-free. Pack a reusable water bottle to stay hydrated in the heat—many beaches and parks have refill stations and showers.

When it comes to mountain terrain, Kauai's trails range from easy walks to challenging hikes, so pack accordingly. Comfortable, moisture-wicking clothing is ideal for staying cool and dry on the trail. For your feet, opt for sturdy hiking shoes or boots with good ankle support, especially if you plan to tackle more difficult trails like the Kalalau Trail on the Na Pali Coast. In wetter areas, trail conditions can be muddy and slippery, so consider bringing gaiters or a change of socks to keep your feet dry.

A small daypack is essential for carrying your gear on hikes. Pack essentials like a first-aid kit, insect repellent, and a small flashlight or headlamp, especially if you're venturing out early in the morning or late in the day. A lightweight rain jacket is also a good idea, as sudden showers are common, particularly in the island's lush interior. Don't forget to bring a map or a fully charged phone with a reliable GPS app if you plan to explore less-traveled trails.

For both beach and mountain excursions, a multi-purpose sarong or beach blanket can be a versatile addition to your packing list. It can serve as a picnic blanket, a quick cover-up, or even a towel in a pinch. If you plan to snorkel, consider bringing your own gear, including a mask, snorkel, and fins, to avoid rental costs and ensure a perfect fit.

Finally, remember to pack a few eco-friendly items to minimize your impact on Kauai's pristine environment. A reusable shopping bag, collapsible cooler, and bamboo utensils can reduce your reliance on single-use plastics. Leave room in your luggage for souvenirs, but also for any trash you might accumulate—Kauai's natural beauty depends on visitors taking care of the island.

Where to Stay and Affordable Accommodations Within a Budget

Finding affordable accommodations in Kauai is key to keeping your trip within budget, and with a bit of research, you can secure a comfortable place to stay without overspending. Kauai offers a range of lodging options, from budget-friendly hotels to vacation rentals and hostels, each with its own advantages depending on your needs and preferences.

Start by exploring vacation rental platforms like Airbnb or Vrbo, which often provide the best value for families or groups. These rentals typically offer more space than a hotel room, plus the added benefit of a kitchen, allowing you to save on meals by cooking some of your own food. Look for rentals in less touristy areas like Kapaa on the East Side or Waimea on the West Side, where prices are generally lower than in the more popular North and South Shores. Booking well in advance can also help you secure the best deals, especially during peak travel seasons.

For solo travelers or those on a tighter budget, hostels are an excellent option. Places like The Kauai Beach House Hostel in Kapa'a offer dormitory-style rooms as well as private rooms at a fraction of the cost of traditional hotels. Hostels also provide a social atmosphere, making them ideal for meeting fellow travelers. Another budget-friendly option is camping, with sites available at state parks like Haena Beach Park and Anahola Beach Park. Just be sure to obtain the necessary permits ahead of time and check the amenities offered at each site, as they vary.

If you prefer the convenience of a hotel, consider staying in a budget-friendly option like Kauai Palms Hotel in Lihue or Tip Top Motel, also in Lihue. These hotels offer basic amenities and are centrally located, making them a great base for exploring the island. While they may not have the luxury of beachfront resorts, they provide clean, comfortable accommodations at a much lower price.

For those who want to be closer to the beach without breaking the bank, consider looking for deals at smaller boutique hotels or older properties that may offer lower rates. The Garden Island Inn in Lihue, for example, is a charming option with colorful rooms and easy access to nearby beaches. Alternatively, consider staying at an all-inclusive resort during off-peak seasons, as they may offer significant discounts that make them more affordable than they appear at first glance.

Another strategy to save on accommodations is to consider staying in a central location like Lihue or Kapa'a, which provides easy access to all parts of the island. This allows you to explore both the North and South Shores without the need to switch accommodations, saving you time and money on transportation. Staying in one location for the duration of your trip can also reduce the stress of packing and unpacking, and some hosts may offer discounts for longer stays.

By carefully selecting your accommodations and considering alternative lodging options, you can enjoy a comfortable stay on Kauai without straining your budget. Remember to book early, especially during high season, and always compare prices across multiple platforms to ensure you're getting the best deal possible. With a bit of planning, you can find the perfect place to rest after a day of exploring the island's natural beauty.

Transportation

Getting around Kauai efficiently while sticking to a budget involves a bit of planning and consideration of your transportation options. While renting a car provides the most flexibility for exploring the island's diverse attractions, there are several other affordable methods to consider, depending on your travel needs.

Rental Cars

Renting a car is often the most convenient option for visitors to Kauai. It allows you to explore the island at your own pace and reach more remote areas that public transportation might not cover. To find the best rates, book your rental car well in advance and compare prices across different companies. Utilize discount websites or apps to check for deals and promotions. Consider renting a car only for part of your trip if you plan to stay in a central location and use other transportation methods for some excursions.

Public Transportation

The Kauai Bus system provides a cost-effective way to get around the island, with routes connecting major towns, popular beaches, and key attractions. Fares are reasonable, typically around $2.50 per ride, and a day pass is available for unlimited travel within a 24-hour period. The bus system is reliable but may not reach all the island's remote areas, so plan your routes and schedules in advance. Check the Kauai Bus website for route maps and schedules to ensure you can navigate effectively.

Ride-Sharing and Taxis

For those who prefer not to rent a car or are only visiting specific areas, ride-sharing services like Uber and Lyft are available in Kauai, though coverage may be limited compared to larger cities. Be prepared for higher fares in more remote areas or during peak times. Taxis are also an option, but they can be more expensive, so consider using them for occasional trips or to get to and from the airport.

Bicycles and Scooter Rentals

Renting a bicycle or scooter is an affordable and fun way to explore towns and nearby attractions. Many areas, such as Kapaa and Hanalei, have bike paths and rental shops where you can rent bikes by the hour or day. This option is particularly suitable for short distances and local sightseeing. If you're comfortable navigating traffic, scooters can be a convenient alternative, but always follow safety guidelines and local traffic laws.

Carpooling and Group Tours

If you're traveling with a group or are interested in specific activities, consider joining group tours or carpooling. Group tours often include transportation as part of the package, which can be cost-effective compared to renting a car for each participant. Look for local tour operators offering shared transportation options for popular destinations and activities, such as scenic drives or hiking trips.

Airport Transportation

For transportation from Lihue Airport (LIH), several options are available. Shuttle services can be pre-booked and are a convenient way to get to your accommodation without the hassle of arranging a rental car immediately. Airport taxis and ride-sharing services are also readily available, though they may be more expensive than pre-arranged shuttles. Some hotels offer complimentary airport transfers, so check with your accommodation to see if this service is included.

How Long Should I Stay?

For a budget-conscious trip, plan to stay 5-7 days. This allows enough time to explore the island's key attractions without feeling rushed. A week gives you the flexibility to balance sightseeing with relaxation, and you'll have time to experience both the North and South Shores. If you're short on time, a 4-day itinerary can still cover the essentials, but you may need to prioritize your must-see spots.

Three to Four Days

If you're on a short trip, three to four days can give you a taste of Kauai's highlights. During this time, focus on exploring key areas such as the North Shore, with its stunning beaches like Hanalei Bay and the dramatic Na Pali Coast, and the South Shore, home to Poipu Beach and the charming town of Koloa. Dedicate a day to experiencing local culture and perhaps visiting a few popular hikes, like the short and rewarding Sleeping Giant Trail. This timeframe allows you to sample the island's diverse offerings but will require prioritizing activities and possibly limiting some experiences.

Five to Seven Days

With a week on the island, you can enjoy a more relaxed pace and explore additional regions. Spend a couple of days in the North Shore and South Shore, taking time to enjoy the beaches, local dining, and sightseeing. Use the remaining days to venture into Kauai's interior, visiting Waimea Canyon—often referred to as the "Grand Canyon of the Pacific"—and the lush landscapes of the East Coast. This duration also provides flexibility for day trips, such as a boat tour along the Na Pali Coast or a visit to the charming town of Hanapepe. A week allows you to experience a broader range of activities and attractions without feeling rushed.

Ten Days or More

For those with ten days or more, Kauai can be thoroughly explored, and you can delve into both well-known and off-the-beaten-path destinations. Spend ample time in each region, such as a few days in the North Shore for hiking and beach relaxation, several days in the South Shore for water activities and local culture, and a few days exploring the interior, including Waimea Canyon and the serene Wailua River area. With this extended timeframe, you can also enjoy additional activities like zip-lining, snorkeling, and visiting more remote beaches. Consider splitting your stay between different regions of the island to reduce travel time and fully immerse yourself in each area's unique offerings.

Regardless of your length of stay, be sure to balance relaxation with exploration. Kauai's laid-back atmosphere is perfect for unwinding, but its diverse landscape also offers a wealth of activities and sights. Plan your itinerary based on your interests—whether it's hiking, beachcombing, or cultural experiences—to make the most of your time on this beautiful island.

2

Getting Settled Once You Arrive

Welcome to Kauai! Now that you've landed on the Garden Isle, it's time to get settled and start making the most of your stay. This chapter is all about helping you get acquainted with the local area, get into your accommodations smoothly, and prepare for the adventures ahead. From finding the best farmers markets and rental services to adjusting to the local wildlife and managing jet lag, we've got you covered. Let's dive in.

Farmers Markets

Kauai's farmers markets are a treasure trove of fresh, local produce, handmade goods, and a great way to experience the island's community vibe. Whether you're stocking up on snacks for your hikes or looking to taste some local flavors, these markets are your go-to spots.

- **When and Where**: Farmers' markets are held almost daily across the island. The largest and most popular is the Kauai Community Market in Lihue, held on Saturdays. Other notable ones include the Hanalei Farmers Market on Saturdays and the Kapa'a Sunshine Market on Wednesdays.

- **What to Expect**: Fresh fruits like papayas, pineapples, and coconuts, as well as vegetables, baked goods, and local delicacies. Don't miss out on trying taro, a staple in Hawaiian cuisine, or grabbing some fresh poke.
- **Tips**: Arrive early to get the best selection, and bring cash, as many vendors do not accept cards.

Rentals (Car, Surfboards, Snorkel Gear, etc.)

To fully explore Kauai, you'll likely need to rent some gear. Whether it's a car to get around or equipment for water activities, here's what you need to know:

- **Car Rentals**: While renting a car is the most convenient way to explore Kauai, it can also be one of the most expensive parts of your trip. Book in advance and look for deals online. Companies like Turo allow you to rent cars directly from owners, often at lower rates. If you're planning to stay in one area, consider renting a car only for the days you need it and using public transportation or biking for the rest.
- **Surfboards and Snorkel Gear**: Local shops in Hanalei, Poipu, and Kapa'a offer affordable daily and weekly rentals. Some accommodations even provide gear for free or at discounted rates. Check if your Airbnb or hotel includes these amenities before renting elsewhere.
- **Bikes and Scooters**: For shorter trips around towns or beaches, consider renting a bike or scooter. It's eco-friendly and can save you money on gas and parking.

Supermarket/Non-Restaurant Food Options

Eating out every day can quickly eat into your budget, but Kauai has plenty of options for affordable, fresh food that you can prepare yourself:

- **Grocery Stores**: Safeway, Foodland, and Costco (if you have a membership) are your best bets for stocking up on essentials. For local products, try the smaller markets like Papaya's Natural Foods in Kapa'a or the Hanalei Natural Food Store.
- **Big-Box Stores**: Walmart, Target and Costco in Lihue offer bulk buying options that are great for families or groups staying for a longer period.
- **Local Markets**: If you prefer to cook with local ingredients, the farmers markets are an excellent choice. Not only will you find fresh produce, but also locally made jams, sauces, and baked goods.

Sea Life to Expect

Kauai's waters are teeming with vibrant marine life, making snorkeling and diving some of the most rewarding activities you can do on a budget.

- **Fish**: Expect to see a variety of colorful fish, such as the state fish of Hawaii, the Humuhumunukunukuāpua'a (triggerfish), and parrotfish. These species are commonly found in snorkeling spots like Tunnels Beach and Poipu Beach.
- **Turtles**: Sea turtles, or honu, are often spotted around the island's beaches. Always remember to observe from a distance and respect these protected animals.
- **Whales and Dolphins**: During the winter months, humpback

whales migrate through the Hawaiian waters. Dolphins can also be seen year-round, especially on boat tours along the Na Pali Coast.

- **Hawaiian Monk Seals**: Just like the sea turtles, Hawaiian monk seals often come up to rest on sandy beaches. It is important to keep your distance but they are beautiful to see up close.

Wildlife to Expect

Kauai's diverse ecosystems are home to a range of wildlife, from high in the trees and low in the bushes, you can spot many diverse animals that are home to Kauai.

- **Birds**: Kauai is a bird-watcher's paradise, with species like the Nēnē (Hawaiian goose) and the vibrant red I'iwi. The Kilauea Point National Wildlife Refuge is a great spot to see some of these species.
- **Mongoose**: You might spot these small, weasel-like creatures darting across roads or through the underbrush. They're an introduced species and can be seen throughout the island.
- **Chickens**: One of Kauai's most iconic sights is its wild chickens. Descendants of domestic chickens that were freed during hurricanes, these birds are everywhere and have become a charming, if noisy, part of the island's character.

Managing Jet Lag

Traveling to Kauai can involve a significant time change, especially if you're coming from the mainland or further afield. Here's how to minimize the impact of jet lag:

- **Before You Arrive**: Start adjusting your sleep schedule a few days before departure by going to bed and waking up an hour earlier or later, depending on where you're coming from.

- **During the Flight**: Stay hydrated, avoid alcohol, and try to sleep according to Kauai's time zone. A neck pillow and eye mask can help you get some rest on the plane.
- **Upon Arrival**: Spend time outdoors in natural light as soon as you arrive. This will help reset your internal clock. Avoid long naps and try to stay awake until a reasonable bedtime to adjust to the new time zone.

Local Shopping Centers

Kauai's shopping centers are more than just places to buy essentials; they're hubs of local culture where you can find everything from groceries to souvenirs.

- **Kukui Grove Center (Lihue)**: The largest shopping center on the island, offering a range of stores including Macy's, Longs Drugs, and a variety of local boutiques. There's also a food court if you're looking for a quick bite.
- **Princeville Shopping Center (North Shore)**: A convenient spot for groceries, banking, and dining. The center includes Foodland, a pharmacy, and several restaurants.
- **Poipu Shopping Village (South Shore)**: Located near popular resorts, this shopping village offers a mix of shops, galleries, and dining options. It's a great place to pick up souvenirs or enjoy a meal after a day at the beach.

Getting settled in Kauai is your first step toward an unforgettable adventure. With this information, you'll be prepared to hit the ground running, whether you're picking up fresh produce at a local market, renting gear for your next adventure, or simply getting to know the island's unique wildlife. Now that you're settled, let's explore what Kauai has to offer.

3

Popular Foods of Kauai

Kauai is not just a feast for the eyes, but also for the taste buds. The island's cuisine is a melting pot of flavors influenced by its rich cultural history, blending Hawaiian traditions with Asian, Portuguese, and American tastes. In this chapter, we'll explore some of the must-try dishes that define the local food scene. From fresh seafood to iconic comfort foods, here's what you need to savor during your stay in Kauai.

Poke

Poke (pronounced poh-kay) is a beloved Hawaiian dish that has gained international fame for its simplicity and freshness. It consists of cubed raw fish, usually ahi tuna, marinated in a variety of seasonings like soy sauce, sesame oil, and seaweed.

- **What It Is**: A raw fish salad, typically served over a bed of rice or as a standalone dish.
- **What It's Made Of**: Fresh ahi tuna, soy sauce, sesame oil, seaweed,

green onions, and occasionally, avocado or spicy mayo.
- **Where to Get the Best**: Head to Koloa Fish Market or The Fish Express in Lihue for some of the freshest poke on the island. Both spots are known for their high-quality fish and traditional preparations.

Poi

Poi is a traditional Hawaiian staple made from the taro plant, which has been cultivated in Hawaii for centuries. This starchy dish might be an acquired taste for some, but it's a must-try to fully experience the local culture.

- **What It Is**: A smooth, purple paste made from pounded taro root, often served as a side dish.
- **What It's Made Of**: Taro root, water, and sometimes a touch of salt.
- **Where to Get the Best**: You can find authentic poi at Hanalei Taro & Juice Co., where it's made fresh and served alongside other traditional Hawaiian foods.

Loco Moco

Loco Moco is the ultimate Hawaiian comfort food, perfect for those looking for a hearty meal. This dish is a true reflection of the island's mixed cultural influences.

- **What It Is**: A savory dish consisting of a hamburger patty served over rice, topped with a fried egg and smothered in rich brown gravy.
- **What It's Made Of**: White rice, ground beef patty, fried egg, and

brown gravy.

- **Where to Get the Best**: Tip Top Motel Café & Bakery in Lihue is a local favorite for Loco Moco. Their version is hearty and full of flavor, making it a popular spot for both locals and visitors.

Saimin

Saimin is a noodle soup that reflects the multicultural heritage of Hawaii. Influenced by Japanese, Chinese, and Filipino cuisine, this dish is a comforting bowl of goodness.

- **What It Is**: A noodle soup similar to ramen, with a light broth and a variety of toppings.
- **What It's Made Of**: Wheat noodles, dashi broth, green onions, kamaboko (fish cake), char siu (barbecue pork), and sometimes egg or vegetables.
- **Where to Get the Best**: Hamura Saimin in Lihue is the go-to spot for authentic saimin. This local institution has been serving up steaming bowls of this delicious soup for decades.

Fish Tacos

Given Kauai's abundant coastline, it's no surprise that fish tacos are a popular dish here. They're light, fresh, and bursting with flavor, making them an ideal choice for a casual meal by the beach.

- **What It Is**: Tacos filled with grilled or fried fish, topped with cabbage, pico de gallo, and a drizzle of creamy sauce.
- **What It's Made Of**: Fresh fish (usually mahi-mahi or ono), corn or flour tortillas, cabbage, pico de gallo, and a creamy or spicy sauce.
- **Where to Get the Best**: Mermaids Café in Kapaa is known for its

flavorful fish tacos, which are made with fresh, local ingredients and served with a unique island twist.

Coconut Shrimp

Coconut shrimp is a popular appetizer in Kauai, combining the island's love for seafood with the tropical flavor of coconut. This dish is crunchy, sweet, and perfect for sharing.

- **What It Is**: Shrimp coated in a crispy coconut batter, fried until golden brown, and often served with a sweet dipping sauce.
- **What It's Made Of**: Shrimp, shredded coconut, flour, eggs, and a sweet dipping sauce (often mango or pineapple-based).
- **Where to Get the Best**: Keoki's Paradise in Poipu offers some of the best coconut shrimp on the island, with a perfect balance of crunch and sweetness.

Spam Musubi

Spam Musubi is a quintessential Hawaiian snack that might seem unusual at first, but it's a local favorite. This portable bite is a fusion of Japanese onigiri and American Spam, making it a unique taste of Hawaii's culinary history.

- **What It Is**: A slice of grilled Spam on top of a block of rice, wrapped with a strip of nori (seaweed).
- **What It's Made Of**: Spam, rice, nori, and sometimes a soy or teriyaki glaze.
- **Where to Get the Best**: You can find Spam Musubi at most convenience stores and local eateries across the island. Ishihara Market in Waimea is particularly known for its delicious take on

this snack. Or if you are out and about, track down The Musubi Truck for musubi on the go.

Kalua Pig

Kalua Pig is a traditional Hawaiian dish that's often the centerpiece of a luau. Slow-cooked to perfection, this smoky, tender pork is a must-try for meat lovers.

- **What It Is**: Slow-cooked, shredded pork with a smoky flavor, traditionally cooked in an underground oven called an imu.
- **What It's Made Of**: Pork shoulder, Hawaiian sea salt, and liquid smoke (if not cooked in an imu).
- **Where to Get the Best**: For an authentic experience, head to a local luau where the Kalua Pig is often prepared the traditional way. For a more casual setting, try Puka Dog in Poipu, which serves Kalua Pig in a Hawaiian-style hot dog.

Lilikoi

Lilikoi, or passion fruit, is a vibrant, tropical fruit that's widely used in Kauai's cuisine. Its sweet-tart flavor is refreshing and can be found in various forms, from juices to desserts.

- **What It Is**: A round, yellow fruit with a juicy, seedy interior, known for its bright, tangy flavor.
- **What It's Made Of**: The pulp and seeds of the lilikoi fruit.
- **Where to Get the Best**: Try a fresh lilikoi smoothie or lilikoi-flavored dessert at Banana Joe's Fruit Stand in Kilauea, pick up some lilikoi from a local farmers market, or enjoy all things lilikoi at Aunty Lilikoi in Waimea for more passion fruit products.

Exploring the popular foods of Kauai is more than just eating—it's about experiencing the island's rich cultural tapestry. Each dish tells a story of the land and the people who have called it home. So, whether you're biting into a fresh poke bowl or savoring the smoky flavor of Kalua Pig, you're getting a taste of Kauai's history, diverse traditions, and aloha spirit.

4

Most Affordable Restaurants in Kauai on a Budget

E xploring Kauai's culinary scene doesn't have to break the bank. Whether you're in Lihue, Wailua, or Kapaʻa, there are plenty of budget-friendly restaurants that offer delicious meals without compromising on quality. In this chapter, we'll guide you through some of the best affordable dining spots, highlighting their most popular dishes and what makes each one special.

Tip Top

Tip Top is a beloved local institution in Lihue that's been serving up hearty meals since 1916. Known for its down-home atmosphere and wallet-friendly prices, it's a great spot to grab breakfast or lunch.

- **Budget-Friendly Rating**: $$
- **Best Dishes**: Try the oxtail soup, which is a local favorite, or their fluffy macadamia nut pancakes topped with coconut syrup. The loco moco, with its generous portions of rice, hamburger patty, egg,

and gravy, is also a must-try.

- **Additional Information**: Tip Top is also a bakery, so don't leave without sampling some of their fresh pastries. The place fills up quickly, so aim to arrive early.

Hamura Saimin Stand

For an authentic taste of local Kauai cuisine, Hamura Saimin Stand in Lihue is a must-visit. This humble eatery specializes in saimin, a Hawaiian noodle soup that's both comforting and affordable.

- **Budget-Friendly Rating**: $
- **Best Dishes**: The saimin, of course, is the star here. It's a simple dish of noodles in a savory broth, topped with green onions, kamaboko (fish cake), and char siu (barbecue pork). Don't miss their lilikoi chiffon pie for dessert.
- **Additional Information**: The atmosphere is no-frills, but that's part of its charm. Expect to share your table with locals and other travelers alike.

Tiki Tacos

Located in Kapaʻa, Tiki Tacos is the place to go for a quick, flavorful, and filling meal. Known for its generous portions and fresh ingredients, this spot is a favorite among both locals and visitors.

- **Budget-Friendly Rating**: $$
- **Best Dishes**: Their fish tacos are legendary, packed with grilled fish, fresh cabbage, and a variety of house-made salsas. The Kalua pork taco is another popular choice, offering a taste of traditional

Hawaiian flavors in a handheld form.

- **Additional Information**: Tiki Tacos offers gluten-free options, and their tacos are big enough to satisfy even the hungriest of appetites.

Pho Kauai

If you're craving something warm and comforting, Pho Kauai in Lihue serves up some of the best Vietnamese noodle soups on the island. It's a great spot for a budget-friendly meal that doesn't skimp on flavor.

- **Budget-Friendly Rating**: $
- **Best Dishes**: The pho, with its rich, aromatic broth, is the main draw here. You can choose from a variety of toppings, including beef, chicken, and tofu. The spring rolls are also a great starter or light snack.
- **Additional Information**: Pho Kauai's casual atmosphere makes it perfect for a quick meal. They also offer takeout if you're in a hurry.

Big Monster Sushi & Rice - Lawai

For sushi lovers, Big Monster Sushi & Rice in Lawai offers fresh, delicious rolls at a fraction of the price you might expect. The portions are generous, and the quality is top-notch, making it a great value for your money.

- **Budget-Friendly Rating**: $$
- **Best Dishes**: The spicy ahi roll and tempura shrimp roll are popular choices, offering a satisfying mix of flavors and textures. They also serve bento boxes, which are perfect for a quick, balanced meal.

- **Additional Information**: The restaurant is small, so it's best to go during off-peak hours to avoid the crowds.

The Fish Express

Another Lihue favorite, The Fish Express, is a go-to spot for fresh, affordable seafood. Whether you're in the mood for poke, plate lunches, or a simple fish sandwich, this place has you covered.

- **Budget-Friendly Rating**: $$
- **Best Dishes**: Their poke bowls are a must-try, featuring fresh ahi tuna seasoned to perfection. The furikake-crusted ahi plate is another standout, served with rice and a choice of sides.
- **Additional Information**: The Fish Express is primarily a takeout spot, so it's perfect for grabbing a quick meal before heading to the beach or back to your hotel.

The Musubi Truck

If you're looking for a quick, portable snack or meal, The Musubi Truck in Wailua is the place to go. Specializing in spam musubi, this food truck offers a taste of Hawaii that's both delicious and easy on the wallet.

- **Budget-Friendly Rating**: $
- **Best Dishes**: The classic spam musubi is a must, but you can also try variations with teriyaki chicken or ahi tuna. They also offer combo plates if you're looking for something more substantial.
- **Additional Information**: The Musubi Truck is often parked in different locations, so check their social media for their daily spot. It's a great option for a quick bite on the go.

Keoki's

Located in Poipu, Keoki's Paradise is a bit more upscale but still offers some affordable options, especially if you stick to their happy hour menu. The tropical atmosphere and live music make it a fun spot to dine without blowing your budget.

- **Budget-Friendly Rating**: $$-$$$
- **Best Dishes**: The fish tacos and coconut shrimp are popular choices, especially during happy hour when the prices are lower. Their Hula Pie, a massive ice cream dessert, is perfect for sharing.
- **Additional Information**: Keoki's can get busy, so reservations are recommended, especially if you're planning to visit during peak dining hours.

The Crooked Surf at the Sheraton Coconut Beach Resort

The Crooked Surf offers a more laid-back dining experience, perfect for those looking to enjoy a meal with a view. Located at the Sheraton Coconut Beach Resort, this spot is known for its beachfront location and reasonably priced dishes.

- **Budget-Friendly Rating**: $$-$$$
- **Best Dishes**: The poke nachos are a must-try, combining fresh ahi tuna with crispy wonton chips and a variety of toppings. The burger and fries are also a solid choice if you're in the mood for something more familiar.
- **Additional Information**: While The Crooked Surf is part of a resort, the prices are surprisingly reasonable, making it a great

option for a more relaxed dining experience.

Passion Bakery Café

For breakfast or a light lunch, Passion Bakery Café in Kapa'a is a fantastic choice. Known for its fresh-baked goods and casual atmosphere, it's a great place to start your day without spending too much.

- **Budget-Friendly Rating**: $
- **Best Dishes**: The lilikoi (passion fruit) glazed donuts are a local favorite, and their breakfast sandwiches are both hearty and affordable. The cinnamon rolls and croissants are also excellent.
- **Additional Information**: Passion Bakery Café is a popular spot, so get there early to ensure you don't miss out on their freshly baked treats.

Paco's Tacos Cantina Kapaa

If you're craving Mexican food, Paco's Tacos Cantina in Kapaa offers tasty, affordable dishes in a vibrant setting. This casual eatery is perfect for a quick, satisfying meal.

- **Budget-Friendly Rating**: $$
- **Best Dishes**: The fish tacos are a standout, offering a fresh, zesty flavor that's perfect for the island vibe. The carnitas burrito and churros are also highly recommended.
- **Additional Information**: Paco's Tacos often has live music, adding to the festive atmosphere. It's a great spot for a fun, affordable night out.

Each of these restaurants offers a unique taste of Kauai without putting a strain on your budget. Whether you're in the mood for traditional Hawaiian dishes, fresh seafood, or something a bit more international, you'll find plenty of options that satisfy both your cravings and your wallet.

5

Locals and Tourists' Favorite Hikes of Kauai

Kauai, often referred to as the "Garden Isle," is a hiker's paradise with its lush landscapes, breathtaking vistas, and a variety of trails that cater to all skill levels. Whether you're seeking a leisurely coastal stroll or a challenging trek through dense jungle terrain, this chapter highlights some of the most beloved hikes on the island, favored by both locals and tourists alike. Each hike offers something unique, from panoramic canyon views to serene waterfalls, making it easy to find a trail that fits your adventure style. We'll cover the essentials, including descriptions of the hikes, their difficulty levels, parking information, and tips to ensure you're well-prepared for your journey.

Mahaulepu Coastal Trail & Cave, Poipu

The Mahaulepu Coastal Trail is a scenic coastal hike that offers stunning views of the rugged southern coastline of Kauai. It's a relatively easy hike, making it accessible for hikers of all skill levels, and it provides a great opportunity to explore the natural beauty of the island.

- **Difficulty Level**: Easy
- **Description**: This 4-mile round-trip hike takes you along the picturesque coastline, where you'll encounter rocky cliffs, secluded beaches, and unique limestone formations. The trail also passes by the Makauwahi Cave, an ancient sinkhole that is now a fascinating archaeological site.
- **Parking**: There's free parking available at Shipwreck Beach, where the trail begins. However, parking can be limited, especially on weekends, so it's a good idea to arrive early.
- **Helpful Advice**: Wear sturdy shoes, as the trail can be rocky in some areas. Bring plenty of water and sunscreen, as there's little shade along the trail. Be sure to explore the Makauwahi Cave, but note that it may be closed during certain hours, so check ahead of time.

The Canyon Trail, Waimea Canyon

Waimea Canyon, often called the "Grand Canyon of the Pacific," is one of Kauai's most iconic natural landmarks. The Canyon Trail offers a moderately challenging hike that rewards you with incredible views of the canyon's vibrant red and green cliffs.

- **Difficulty Level**: Moderate
- **Description**: This 3.4-mile round-trip trail winds through the Waimea Canyon State Park, offering breathtaking views of the canyon and surrounding landscape. The trail culminates at the Waipoo Falls, a 800-foot waterfall that cascades into a lush, tropical valley below.
- **Parking**: There's a parking lot at the Pu'u Hinahina Lookout, which serves as the trailhead. There is a parking fee, so be prepared to pay a small amount.

- **Helpful Advice**: The trail can be steep and slippery, especially after rain, so wear appropriate footwear with good traction. It's also recommended to bring a hat and plenty of water, as the trail can get hot during midday. Start early to avoid the afternoon heat and the crowds.

The Secret Falls, Wailua River

For a more adventurous and unique hiking experience, the trail to Secret Falls (Uluwehi Falls) combines a scenic kayak trip with a moderate hike through a tropical forest, leading you to a beautiful waterfall hidden in the jungle.

- **Difficulty Level**: Moderate
- **Description**: The journey begins with a kayak paddle up the Wailua River, followed by a 1.5-mile hike through lush jungle terrain. The trail can be muddy and involves crossing streams, but the reward is a stunning waterfall where you can cool off with a refreshing swim.
- **Parking**: You can park at the Wailua Marina or Smith's Tropical Paradise, where you can rent kayaks for the trip. Some kayak rental companies include parking in their rental fee.
- **Helpful Advice**: This hike requires some planning, as you'll need to rent a kayak to access the trail. Wear water shoes or sandals, as the trail involves multiple stream crossings. Be prepared for muddy conditions, especially after rain, and don't forget to bring insect repellent.

Sleeping Giant: Nounou East Trailhead

The Sleeping Giant, or Nounou Mountain, offers one of the most popular hikes on Kauai, with panoramic views of the eastern side of the island. The trail is moderately challenging and provides a rewarding trek to the "giant's head."

- **Difficulty Level**: Moderate
- **Description**: This 3.4-mile round-trip hike ascends through a forested trail before reaching the summit, where you'll be treated to expansive views of Wailua, Kapaa, and the surrounding ocean. The trail is named for the mountain's profile, which resembles a sleeping giant.
- **Parking**: There's a small parking lot at the Nounou East Trailhead, just off Haleilio Road in Wailua. Parking is free, but spaces are limited, so it's best to arrive early.
- **Helpful Advice**: The trail can be steep and rocky in sections, so wear sturdy shoes with good grip. The summit is often windy, so bring a light jacket. Start your hike early to avoid the heat and enjoy the views before the afternoon clouds roll in.

Makaleha Trailhead

For experienced hikers looking for a challenge, the Makaleha Trail offers a rugged and remote adventure through dense jungle terrain. This trail is less traveled but provides a true wilderness experience, complete with streams, waterfalls, and lush vegetation.

- **Difficulty Level**: Difficult
- **Description**: The Makaleha Trail is a 3-mile round-trip hike that

takes you deep into the Makaleha Mountains. The trail is often overgrown and involves multiple stream crossings, making it a challenging but rewarding trek. Along the way, you'll encounter waterfalls and pristine swimming holes, perfect for a refreshing dip.

- **Parking**: Parking is available at the end of Kahuna Road in Kapa'a, near the trailhead. The road can be rough, so it's recommended to drive a vehicle with higher clearance.
- **Helpful Advice**: This hike is not for beginners, as the trail can be difficult to follow and involves navigating through dense vegetation. Wear long pants and bring plenty of water and snacks, as this hike can take several hours. It's also a good idea to bring a GPS or a detailed trail map, as the trail can be hard to follow in places.

Each of these hikes offers a unique way to experience the natural beauty of Kauai. Whether you're looking for a leisurely walk along the coast or a challenging trek through the jungle, you'll find a trail that fits your style. Remember to always hike responsibly, respect the natural environment, and be prepared for the varying conditions you may encounter.

6

Best Beaches on the Island

K auai's coastline is a breathtaking mix of golden sands, dramatic cliffs, and turquoise waters. The island is home to some of Hawaii's most stunning and diverse beaches, each offering a unique experience. Whether you're in search of a peaceful spot to sunbathe, a beach with excellent snorkeling, or a stretch of sand perfect for watching the sunset, this chapter will guide you through the best beaches on Kauai. We'll cover where each beach is located, what activities are recommended, parking information, and some helpful tips to make the most of your visit.

Poipu Beach

Poipu Beach, located on the sunny south shore of Kauai, is often considered one of the island's most popular beaches, especially for families. Its calm waters, abundant marine life, and convenient amenities make it an excellent spot for a day of fun in the sun.

- **Location**: South Shore, Poipu
- **Recommended Activities**: Snorkeling, swimming, sunbathing,

picnicking, and turtle watching. Poipu Beach is also a great spot for beginner surfers due to its gentle waves.

- **Parking**: There's a large free parking lot adjacent to the beach, but it can fill up quickly during peak hours. Arrive early to secure a spot.
- **Helpful Advice**: The beach has a protected cove, ideal for young children and novice swimmers. The western side of the beach is known for its snorkeling, where you can spot Hawaiian green sea turtles and colorful fish. Restrooms, showers, and picnic tables are available, making it a convenient spot for a full day out.

Polihale State Park

If you're seeking a remote and uncrowded beach experience, Polihale State Park on Kauai's west side offers miles of pristine, sandy coastline. This beach is perfect for those who love adventure and don't mind the journey to get there.

- **Location**: West Shore, Polihale
- **Recommended Activities**: Sunbathing, beachcombing, camping, and watching the sunset. Swimming is not recommended due to strong currents.
- **Parking**: Parking is available near the beach, but getting there requires a drive down a bumpy, unpaved road. A 4WD vehicle is highly recommended.
- **Helpful Advice**: Polihale's isolation means you'll have plenty of space to yourself, but it also means there are no facilities nearby. Bring everything you need, including plenty of water, snacks, and shade. The sunsets here are spectacular, so plan to stay until dusk if you can.

Kekaha Beach Park

Kekaha Beach Park is a long stretch of sand on Kauai's west side, known for its striking views of the Na Pali Coast and the island of Niihau. This beach is less crowded than others and offers a peaceful escape.

- **Location**: West Shore, Kekaha
- **Recommended Activities**: Sunbathing, beachcombing, and watching the sunset. Like Polihale, swimming is not recommended due to strong currents.
- **Parking**: There's ample parking available right by the beach, and it's usually easy to find a spot.
- **Helpful Advice**: The beach is ideal for a quiet day of relaxation, but bring your own shade as there are few trees or shelters. The sunsets are particularly beautiful here, making it a great spot to end your day.

Salt Pond Beach Park

Salt Pond Beach Park is a family-friendly beach on the west side of Kauai, offering calm waters, picnic areas, and nearby tide pools to explore. It's a great spot for a laid-back beach day.

- **Location**: West Shore, Hanapepe
- **Recommended Activities**: Swimming, snorkeling, tide pooling, and picnicking.
- **Parking**: There's a large parking lot with plenty of space, and it's close to the beach.
- **Helpful Advice**: The beach is named after the traditional Hawaiian salt ponds nearby, where locals still harvest salt. The water is calm and perfect for children. Tide pools at the eastern end of the beach

are fun to explore, especially for young ones. Facilities include restrooms, showers, and picnic tables.

Glass Beach

Glass Beach, located near Port Allen on the southern coast, is a unique and small beach famous for its colorful sea glass that has been worn smooth by the ocean.

- **Location**: South Shore, Port Allen
- **Recommended Activities**: Beachcombing and photography. Swimming is not recommended due to the rocky shore.
- **Parking**: There's limited street parking near the beach. It's a short walk from the road to the beach.
- **Helpful Advice**: Glass Beach is best visited during low tide when more sea glass is visible. The beach is small, and the sea glass can vary depending on the tides and recent weather, but it's worth a visit for the unique photo opportunities. Remember to leave the glass behind for others to enjoy.

Kapa'a Beach Park

Kapa'a Beach Park is a small, centrally located beach on the eastern shore of Kauai, known for its convenience and views of the surrounding area. It's a good spot to relax and watch the waves.

- **Location**: East Shore, Kapa'a
- **Recommended Activities**: Picnicking, fishing, and beachcombing.
- **Parking**: There's a small parking lot near the beach, and it's usually easy to find a spot.

- **Helpful Advice**: The beach is close to the shops and restaurants of Kapa'a, making it easy to grab a bite or explore the town after your beach visit. The water can be rough, so swimming isn't recommended, but it's a nice spot for a peaceful break.

Keālia Beach

Keālia Beach is a long, sandy beach on the eastern coast, popular with both locals and visitors for its consistent waves, making it a great spot for surfers.

- **Location**: East Shore, Kapa'a
- **Recommended Activities**: Surfing, bodyboarding, and sunbathing. Swimming is possible, but the waves can be strong.
- **Parking**: There's a large parking lot right by the beach, so finding a spot is usually easy.
- **Helpful Advice**: Keālia Beach is one of the best spots on the island for surfing, with waves suitable for both beginners and experienced surfers. Lifeguards are often on duty, making it safer for those who want to swim or bodyboard. Bring plenty of sunscreen, as shade is limited.

Kauapea Beach

Known as "Secret Beach," Kauapea Beach is a hidden gem on the north shore of Kauai, offering seclusion and stunning views. It's a bit of a trek to get to, but the beauty of the beach makes it well worth the effort.

- **Location**: North Shore, near Kilauea
- **Recommended Activities**: Sunbathing, beachcombing, and photography. Swimming is not recommended due to strong currents.

- **Parking**: There's limited parking at the end of a dirt road near the trailhead. The hike to the beach is about 10-15 minutes downhill.
- **Helpful Advice**: Kauapea Beach is a secluded spot, so be prepared for a bit of a hike to get there. The beach is clothing-optional in some areas, so be aware of that if you're visiting with family. Bring your own water and snacks, as there are no facilities. The beach is stunning, especially in the early morning or late afternoon when the light is soft.

Hanalei Pavilion Beach Park

Hanalei Pavilion Beach Park is one of the most iconic beaches on the north shore, known for its stunning mountain backdrop and calm waters, making it a perfect spot for families.

- **Location**: North Shore, Hanalei Bay
- **Recommended Activities**: Swimming, paddleboarding, kayaking, and sunbathing.
- **Parking**: There's a parking lot close to the beach, but it can fill up quickly, especially on weekends. Arrive early to secure a spot.
- **Helpful Advice**: Hanalei Bay is one of the safest spots for swimming on the island, with gentle waves and a soft sandy bottom. The beach is large, so even on busy days, it's easy to find a quiet spot. There are restrooms, showers, and picnic tables available, making it an ideal spot for a full day at the beach.

Each of these beaches offers a unique experience, whether you're looking for adventure, relaxation, or simply a beautiful place to enjoy the Hawaiian sunshine. Remember to respect the natural environment, follow local guidelines, and always be mindful of ocean conditions when visiting Kauai's beaches.

7

Day Trips That Won't Break the Bank

Kauai is a fantastic place for day trips that offer a mix of activities, food, and beautiful scenery without spending too much. This chapter provides you with three budget-friendly day trips, each focused on a different region of the island. These itineraries are designed to give you a full day of experiences, including the best places to eat, must-see spots, and recommended activities. Whether you're on the North, South, East, or West side of the island, these day trips will help you maximize your time and money.

North Shore Day Trip

The North Shore is known for its lush landscapes and iconic beaches. Here's a practical itinerary to help you explore this beautiful area.

- **Breakfast**: Start your day at Hanalei Bread Company. It's a good choice for a quick and filling breakfast with options like sandwiches and coffee.
- **Morning Activity**: Visit the Hanalei Valley Lookout for a great view of the valley. Then, head to Limahuli Garden and Preserve to

see native Hawaiian plants and learn about the island's history.

- **Lunch**: Stop at Tahiti Nui in Hanalei for a casual meal. Their poke bowls and kalua pork are solid options if you want to try something local.
- **Afternoon Activity**: Spend your afternoon at Hanalei Bay Beach. You can swim, rent a kayak, or just relax. If you're up for a hike, start the Kalalau Trail at Ke'e Beach, but even a short hike gives you a taste of the Na Pali Coast.
- **Dinner**: Wrap up your day with a meal at The Dolphin Restaurant. It's known for fresh fish and a relaxed atmosphere.
- **Practical Tips**: North Shore weather can change quickly, so check the forecast and road conditions before you go.

Polihale State Park Day Trip

Polihale State Park offers a remote beach experience on the West side of Kauai. This day trip is great if you want to explore some of the island's less crowded areas.

- **Breakfast**: Grab breakfast at Kalaheo Café & Coffee Company. It's a convenient stop on your way west, with good coffee and breakfast options.
- **Morning Activity**: Drive to Waimea Canyon and visit several lookouts like Puu Hinahina and Waimea Canyon Overlook. These spots offer excellent views without requiring much walking.
- **Lunch**: Wrangler's Steakhouse in Waimea is a good place for a quick lunch. They serve local dishes like Hawaiian plate lunches, which are affordable and filling.
- **Afternoon Activity**: Head to Polihale State Park. The road there is rough, so a 4WD vehicle is ideal. Once at the beach, you can relax, take a walk, or just enjoy the quiet. Note that swimming can be

dangerous due to strong currents.

- **Dinner**: Bring a packed dinner or head back to Waimea for a simple meal at Island Taco.
- **Practical Tips**: Polihale is remote with no facilities, so bring everything you need, including water and snacks. Bathrooms are located near the camping grounds.

South Shore Day Trip

The South Shore is a popular destination with plenty of sunshine and accessible beaches. This itinerary combines a few key sights with beach time and local eats.

- **Breakfast**: Start your day at Little Fish Coffee in Poipu. They serve good smoothie bowls and coffee, which are perfect for a quick breakfast.
- **Morning Activity**: Visit Spouting Horn, a quick stop to see a natural blowhole. Then, spend your morning at Poipu Beach, where you can swim or snorkel.
- **Lunch**: Grab lunch at Da Crack in Poipu. It's a popular takeout spot known for burritos and tacos. You can take your food to a nearby park or beach.
- **Afternoon Activity**: Visit Allerton Garden or McBryde Garden for a guided tour. These gardens offer a nice break from the beach and a chance to learn about local plants.
- **Dinner**: End your day with dinner at Keoki's Paradise. It's a bit more lively with island-inspired dishes and often live music.
- **Practical Tips**: The South Shore is usually sunny, so don't forget sunscreen and water.

East Shore Day Trip

The East Shore, also called the Coconut Coast, is a mix of local culture, beaches, and easy hikes. This day trip is perfect for those who want a relaxed yet varied day.

- **Breakfast**: Java Kai in Kapa'a is a good spot to start your day. They offer breakfast items like acai bowls and coffee.
- **Morning Activity**: Hike the Sleeping Giant (Nounou Mountain) via the Nounou East Trail. It's a moderate hike that's manageable and offers good views.
- **Lunch**: Stop by Kountry Kitchen in Kapa'a for lunch. Their menu has plenty of local favorites, and the portions are large.
- **Afternoon Activity**: Spend your afternoon at Lydgate Beach Park. It's a safe spot for snorkeling, especially for families. Another option is to rent a kayak or take a boat tour on the Wailua River.
- **Dinner**: Finish your day with dinner at Hukilau Lanai. It's a bit more upscale but offers great local dishes and views.
- **Practical Tips**: The East Shore has many local attractions, so consider adding a visit to the Coconut Marketplace or attending a Smith Family Garden Luau.

These day trips offer a balanced mix of Kauai's natural beauty, local food, and activities, all while keeping your budget in mind. Whether you're exploring the island's rugged coasts or its sun-soaked beaches, these itineraries will help you make the most of your visit.

8

Best Family Activities on a Budget

K auai offers a wide range of activities perfect for families looking to enjoy the island without spending too much. From adventurous outings to laid-back tours, this chapter covers options that cater to all age groups. You'll find activities with cost ranges, booking information, and preparation tips to help you make the most of your trip. These activities are designed to be both fun and affordable, ensuring that your family can create lasting memories while staying within budget.

Self-Guided Audio Driving Tour in Kauai by GuideAlong

Explore Kauai at your own pace with this budget-friendly audio driving tour, which provides commentary about the island's history, culture, and must-see spots.

- **Cost**: $
- **Booking Information**: Purchase online through the GuideAlong website or app. Once downloaded, the tour can be accessed offline.
- **Preparation Tips**: Ensure your car's audio system is compatible with your device, or bring a Bluetooth speaker. Pack snacks and drinks, and plan your stops using the tour's suggested itinerary.

Wailua River & Waterfalls Kayak Tour: Expert-Guided Adventure

Paddle down the scenic Wailua River and explore hidden waterfalls on this guided adventure, perfect for nature-loving families.

- **Cost**: $$$
- **Booking Information**: Reserve your spot through a tour operator like Kayak Kauai. Book in advance, especially during peak seasons.
- **Preparation Tips**: Wear water-resistant clothing and sturdy shoes. Bring a waterproof bag, sunscreen, and bug spray.

Kauai Mountain Tubing Adventure

Float down old plantation canals in a unique tubing adventure surrounded by Kauai's lush landscape. This activity is great for kids and adults alike.

- **Cost**: $$
- **Booking Information**: Book through Kauai Backcountry Adventures. Early booking is recommended due to limited availability.
- **Preparation Tips**: Wear a swimsuit or quick-dry clothing and secure water shoes. Bring a towel and a change of clothes for after the tour.

Wailua Secret Falls Kayak Hike Adventure

Combine kayaking and hiking to discover the beautiful Secret Falls, offering a mix of adventure and natural beauty.

- **Cost**: $$
- **Booking Information**: Available through local companies like Kayak Wailua. Look for deals or family packages.
- **Preparation Tips**: Dress in water-friendly clothing and bring essentials like sunscreen, bug spray, and a waterproof bag. Wear hiking sandals or sturdy shoes.

1.5-2 Hour Guided Waterfall Hike and Swim Tour

Enjoy a shorter, yet thrilling, adventure with a guided waterfall hike and swim tour, perfect for families with younger children.

- **Cost**: $$

- **Booking Information**: Offered by local tour companies, with varying prices. Check for the best deals.
- **Preparation Tips**: Bring swimwear, towels, and plenty of water. Consider a camera or waterproof phone case for photos.

Kauai Surfing Group Lessons

Experience the thrill of learning to surf in a group setting, with lessons designed for beginners and families.

- **Cost**: $$
- **Booking Information**: Book through surf schools like Kauai Surf School or Hawaiian Surfing Adventures. Look for family packages or group discounts.
- **Preparation Tips**: Wear a rash guard or swim shirt. Most schools provide the necessary equipment, but double-check ahead of time.

Kilohana Plantation Train Tour (40 Min.)

This 40-minute train ride offers a fun and educational experience as you tour a working plantation, perfect for a relaxed family outing.

- **Cost**: $
- **Booking Information**: Purchase tickets at Kilohana Plantation or online. Multiple daily tours are available.
- **Preparation Tips**: No special preparation is needed, but bring a hat and sunscreen if you plan to explore the grounds afterward.

These activities offer a mix of adventure, education, and relaxation, all while keeping your budget in check. Whether you're exploring waterfalls or taking a scenic train ride, these experiences will help make your Kauai vacation memorable without overspending.

9

Best Surf/Snorkeling Spots and Rentals

Kauai is home to some of the most stunning surf and snorkel spots in Hawaii, offering a variety of experiences for all skill levels. Whether you're a seasoned surfer or a beginner looking to snorkel in crystal-clear waters, this chapter will guide you to the best locations on the island. We'll cover why each spot is popular, what skill level is required, nearby rental options, and any additional tips that will enhance your experience.

PK's/Centers

PK's, also known as Prince Kuhio's, is a famous surf spot on the South Shore known for its consistent waves and beautiful reef.

- **Skill Level**: Intermediate to Advanced
- **Why It's Popular**: Reliable waves, scenic surroundings, and a vibrant local surf culture make PK's a favorite among experienced surfers.
- **Rentals Nearby**: Several surf shops in the Poipu area offer board rentals, such as Nukumoi Surf Co.

- **Additional Information**: The reef can be sharp, so it's recommended to wear reef-safe booties. Be mindful of the strong currents and other surfers in the water.

Shipwreck Beach

Located near the Grand Hyatt, Shipwreck Beach offers powerful waves and a stunning backdrop, making it a popular spot for both surfing and bodyboarding.

- **Skill Level**: Advanced
- **Why It's Popular**: Known for its large swells, especially during winter months, Shipwreck Beach attracts thrill-seekers looking for challenging surf.
- **Rentals Nearby**: Surfboards can be rented from nearby Poipu Beach rental shops.
- **Additional Information**: Not recommended for beginners due to strong currents and rocky shorelines. Great for experienced surfers looking for a challenge.

Hanalei Bay

This iconic North Shore location is perfect for surfers of all levels and offers some of the best snorkeling on calm days.

- **Skill Level**: Beginner to Advanced
- **Why It's Popular**: Hanalei Bay's crescent-shaped beach offers gentle waves for beginners, while outer breaks cater to more experienced surfers. The clear, calm waters make it ideal for snorkeling as well.
- **Rentals Nearby**: Board and snorkel gear rentals are available from

shops in Hanalei town, such as Hanalei Surf Company.

- **Additional Information**: Early mornings are less crowded, and the scenery is breathtaking. Check the weather conditions, as the bay can get rough during winter.

Kealia Beach

A long, sandy beach on the East Shore, Kealia is known for its consistent surf and is popular with both locals and visitors.

- **Skill Level**: Intermediate to Advanced
- **Why It's Popular**: Kealia offers consistent waves, especially in the summer, and is a great spot for surfing and bodyboarding.
- **Rentals Nearby**: Surfboard rentals are available in nearby Kapaa, with shops like Coconut Coasters offering a range of options.
- **Additional Information**: The beach has lifeguards, making it a safer option for less experienced surfers. The strong currents, however, mean it's best for those with some surf experience.

Polihale

Polihale is a remote beach on the island's west side, offering a long stretch of sand and a serene, uncrowded atmosphere.

- **Skill Level**: Intermediate to Advanced
- **Why It's Popular**: The isolation of Polihale makes it a peaceful spot for surfing and enjoying the natural beauty of Kauai. The waves can be large and powerful.
- **Rentals Nearby**: Due to its remote location, it's best to bring your gear. There are no nearby rental shops.
- **Additional Information**: The road to Polihale can be rough, so a

4WD vehicle is recommended. Pack plenty of water and sunscreen, as there are no facilities nearby.

Poipu Beach

Poipu Beach, located on the South Shore, is one of Kauai's most popular beaches, offering excellent snorkeling and beginner-friendly surf.

- **Skill Level**: Beginner to Intermediate
- **Why It's Popular**: With gentle waves and clear waters, Poipu is great for beginners learning to surf and families looking to snorkel in a safe environment.
- **Rentals Nearby**: Multiple rental options in Poipu, including surfboards, snorkel gear, and even stand-up paddleboards.
- **Additional Information**: The beach has lifeguards, restrooms, and picnic areas. Arrive early to secure parking, as it can get crowded.

Waikoko's

Located near Hanalei, Waikoko's is a less crowded surf spot that offers consistent waves and beautiful scenery.

- **Skill Level**: Intermediate to Advanced
- **Why It's Popular**: This spot is a hidden gem for those looking to escape the crowds of more popular beaches. The waves are consistent, and the location offers stunning views of the North Shore.
- **Rentals Nearby**: Rent surfboards in Hanalei town before heading to Waikoko's.
- **Additional Information**: Parking is limited, and the beach is somewhat secluded, so plan accordingly. The waves here are

powerful, so it's best suited for those with experience.

Kauai's surf and snorkel spots offer something for everyone, whether you're catching waves or exploring the underwater world. With these locations, you'll experience the best the island has to offer, all while staying within your skill level and budget.

10

Conclusion

As you prepare to embark on your Kauai adventure, remember that exploring this beautiful island on a budget doesn't mean compromising on experiences. From breathtaking hikes and pristine beaches to delicious local foods and thrilling activities, Kauai offers a wealth of opportunities to create unforgettable memories without stretching your wallet. This guide aims to provide you with practical tips and insider knowledge to make your trip both enjoyable and affordable.

You've learned about the best places to stay, how to navigate the island, and the top spots for surfing, snorkeling, and dining. Each chapter was designed to help you maximize your time on the island while keeping expenses in check. With this information at your fingertips, you can focus on soaking up the sun, savoring the local cuisine, and exploring the diverse landscapes that make Kauai a tropical paradise.

As you pack your bags and head for the island, remember that the key to a successful budget-friendly trip is planning and flexibility. Stay open to new experiences, and don't hesitate to seek out local recommendations.

Kauai is a place of natural beauty and cultural richness, and it's waiting to offer you a unique and rewarding adventure.

If this guide has helped you in your journey, we'd love to hear about your experience. Please consider leaving a review on Amazon to share your thoughts and help other travelers make the most of their Kauai adventures. Your feedback is invaluable and contributes to making this guide even better for future readers.

Thank you for choosing this book to assist you in your travels. Have a fantastic trip, and may your Kauai adventure be filled with joy, discovery, and cherished memories.

References

Alicia. (2019, September 12). *A Kauai hiking guide for the first time visitor | Kauai, Hawaii*. Miles Less Traveled. https://mileslesstraveled.com/kauai-hiking-guide/

Anderson, S. (2024, June 18). The Ultimate Guide to surfing in Kauai. *AmericanSurfMagazine*. https://www.americansurfmagazine.com/article/kauai-surf-guide

Calderon, A. (2018, June 27). *19 things you Must Eat in Kauai, Hawaii*. BuzzFeed. https://www.buzzfeed.com/ariellecalderon/kauai-eats

Landing, K. (n.d.). *13 Unique Foods to Try in Kauai*. Koloa Landing Resort. https://koloalandingresort.com/unique-foods-try-vacation-kauai

Menu | Big Monster Sushi | Ocean to Table" put all love and energy, to served freshest ingredients to the food lover. (n.d.). Big Monster Sushi. https://www.bigmonstersushi.com/menu

Paco's Tacos Cantina - Kapolei, HI. (n.d.). https://pacostacoskauai.com/

Passion Bakery Cafe. (2024, January 29). *Welcome – Passion Bakery Cafe*. https://www.passionbakeries.com/

Surfing guide to Kauai, Hawaii. (2024, February 2). My Wave Finder. https://www.mywavefinder.com/destination/kauai-hawaii-surf-guide/

The Crooked Surf at the Sheraton Coconut Beach Resort - Kapa'a, HI on OpenTable. (2024, July 8). OpenTable. https://www.opentable.com/restaurant/profile/1294858?ref=1068

Tripadvisor. (n.d.). *THE 10 BEST Day Trips from Kauai (UPDATED*

2024) - Tripadvisor. https://www.tripadvisor.com/Attractions-g29218-Activities-c63-a_sort.PRICE__5F__LOW__5F__TO__5F__HIGH-Kauai_Hawaii.html

Wailua Secret Falls Kayak and Hike 4.5 hour | Kauai.com. (2024, July 11). KAUAI.com. https://www.kauai.com/kauai-tours/wailua-river-waterfall-kayak-adventure

Yelp. (n.d.). *Yelp*. https://www.yelp.com/

30086084R00046